Easy to Make Bible Crafts for Kids

Dear Parents and Teachers:

This book is intended to encourage children to learn Bible stories from the Old and New Testaments. Read each story summary and discuss the lesson with your child or classroom. The easy-to-make Bible crafts reinforce the lessons as the hands-on learning experiences will make learning about God's Word fun! Feel free to copy the patterns ahead of time for your child or classroom. Many crafts may be made using just crayons and scissors! Be creative and enjoy spending time learning more about the Bible!

Sincerely,

Kim Thompson
Karen Hilderbrand

Kim Thompson
Karen Hilderbrand
Twin Sisters Productions

Credits:

Written By: Kim Mitzo Thompson,
Karen Mitzo Hilderbrand
Craft Illustrations: Jackie Binder
Book Design: Kelli Payto
Illustrations By: Mernie Gallagher-Cole

If you do not have access to a copier, you can print off the patterns in this book when you download the FREE Bible Songs album!

Promo code found on page 6.

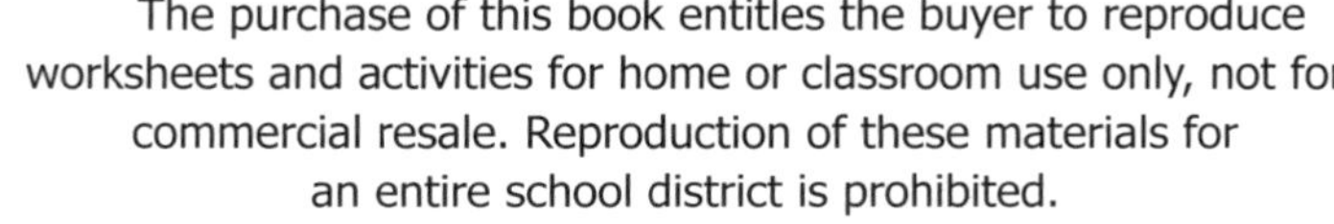

In the Beginning

Genesis 1–2

Lesson: God is good because He made everything including me!

God is our creator and made everything in the entire world. From the smallest of creatures to the huge blue whale, God is perfect in all of His creations. Read below to learn what God made each day.

First Day
God made light which He called "day" and He made darkness which He called "night." And there was evening and there was morning the first day.

Second Day
God made the sky.

Third Day
God made the majestic mountains and the vast oceans. Then He made the beautiful flowers and trees.

Fourth Day
God made the sun, moon and stars.

Fifth Day
God made the fish to fill the oceans and He made birds to fly in the blue skies.

Sixth Day
God made all of the animals like elephants, tigers and tiny bunnies, too. Then God made the first man named Adam. Then God created Eve so Adam would not be alone.

Seventh Day
"By the seventh day God had finished the work he had been doing; so on the seventh day he rested from all his work."
Genesis 2:2

God Is Creator

Make a treat box to share with someone

Materials Needed:
- Pattern
- Crayons or markers
- Scissors
- Candy

Instructions:
1. Color pattern and cut out.
2. Fold on the dotted lines.
3. Cut the dotted lines at the top circles making sure to only cut halfway.
4. Put a candy inside and secure by matching the top slits.

GOD IS THE CREATOR!
Add a piece of your favorite candy to the inside before you share with a friend!
Fold on dotted lines.
Cut on dotted line only halfway through the card.

The Story of Noah Genesis 6-9

Lesson: Noah obeyed God and God kept Noah and his family safe inside the ark.

Genesis 6:9 tells us that "Noah was a righteous man, blameless among the people of his time, and he walked with God." It is amazing that God knew Noah's heart and picked him from all the people living on earth to be the one to build His ark. And, it is also amazing that Noah listened to God and was faithful. Noah, along with his three sons Shem, Ham, and Japheth built a huge boat with three decks exactly as God had directed him. The ark was 450 feet long, 75 feet wide and 45 feet high. Once the ark was complete, God instructed Noah to take two of all living creatures, male and female, and keep them with him on the ark. Then God commanded the skies to break forth with rain. It rained and rained for 40 days and 40 nights. Water covered the entire earth. Noah, his family, and all of the animals were safe inside the ark.

When the rain stopped, a dove brought Noah an olive branch. This meant it was finally safe to leave the ark. So Noah, along with his family, left the ark with all of the animals. Noah built an altar to the Lord and thanked Him for keeping them safe. The Lord was pleased and said that He would never destroy the earth again. And God said, "This is the sign of the covenant I am making between me and you and every living creature with you, a covenant for all generations to come: I have set my rainbow in the clouds, and it will be the sign of the covenant between me and the earth."
Genesis 9:12-14

Rainbow

Materials Needed:

- Pattern
- Crayons or markers
- Scissors
- Cotton balls
- Glue
- String

Instructions:

1. Color pattern and cut out.
2. Glue cotton balls on bottom for clouds.
3. If hanging, punch a hole in the top and tie on string, (optional).

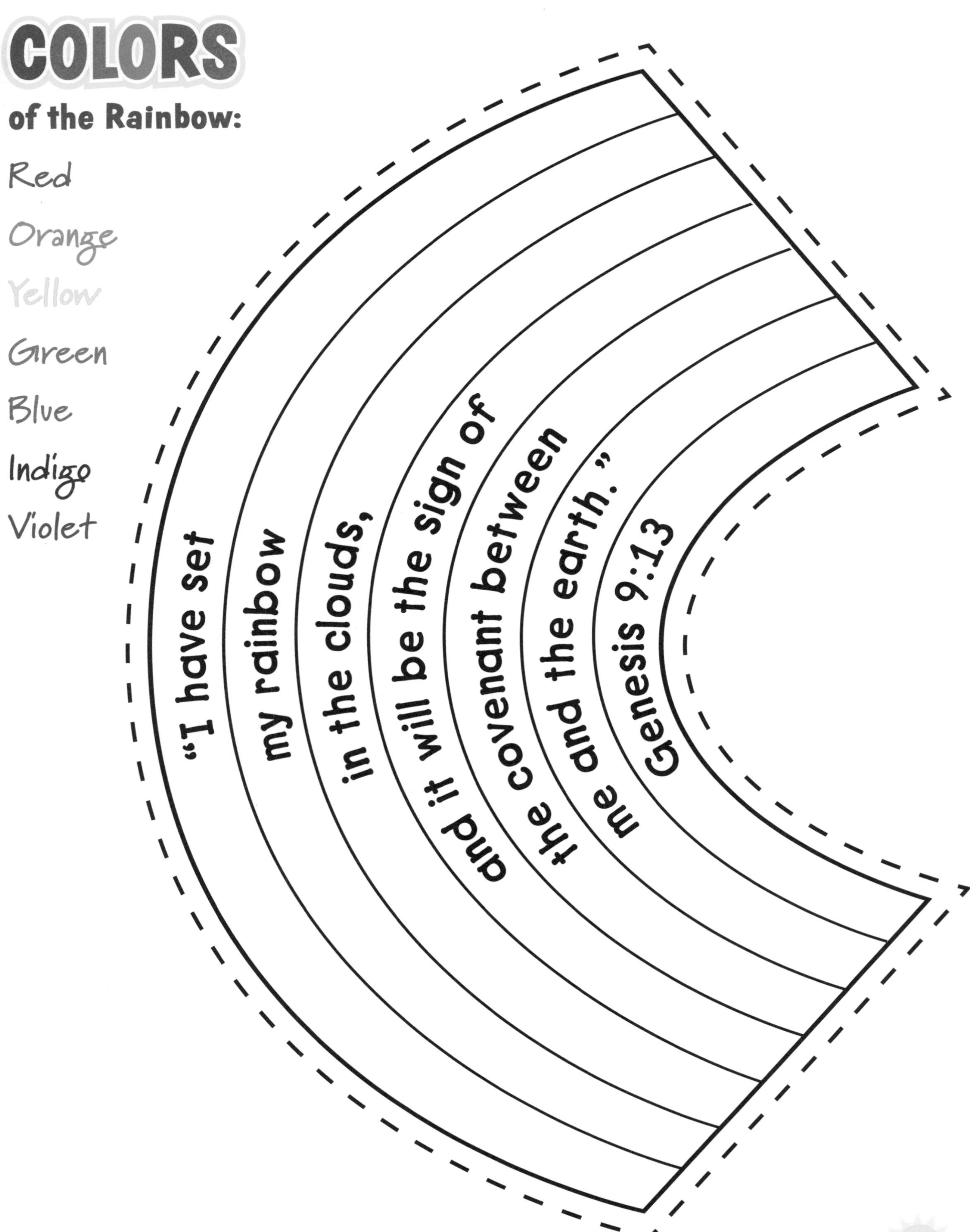
COLORS
of the Rainbow:
Red
Orange
Yellow
Green
Blue
Indigo
Violet
"I have set
my rainbow
in the clouds,
and it will be the sign of
the covenant between
me and the earth."
Genesis 9:13

Joseph's Coat of Many Colors Genesis 37:1-11

Lesson: God is with me even during hard times.

Jacob had twelve sons. But Jacob's youngest son Joseph was his favorite. He gave him presents that he did not give his other sons, including a beautiful robe. This made Joseph's brothers very angry and they became even more jealous of Joseph. One day Joseph told his brothers about a dream he had. He said, "We were in the fields binding bundles of grain together when suddenly my bundle rose up and stood upright while your bundles gathered around mine and bowed down to it." His brothers were angry and said, "Do you intend to rule over us?" This made them hate Joseph even more.

One day Jacob asked Joseph to go check on his brothers in the fields. When Joseph's brothers saw him coming toward them wearing the beautiful robe, they began to make plans to kill him. But the oldest brother Rueben stopped their plan. So they decided to throw Joseph into a pit.

When the brothers saw a caravan of Egyptian merchants pass by they decided to sell Joseph to them as a slave for 20 pieces of silver. Joseph's brothers killed a young goat, dipped Joseph's coat into the blood and told Jacob that they had found the coat on their way home. Jacob wept bitterly and could not be comforted because he thought Joseph was killed by a wild animal. But, God did not forget Joseph. He had a plan for Joseph's life.

Joseph's Coat of Many Colors

Materials Needed:

- Pattern
- Crayons or markers
- Scissors
- Glue
- Pipe cleaners

Instructions:

1. Color pattern and cut out.
2. Glue pipe cleaners to make Joseph's coat colorful.
3. Allow plenty of dry time.

Joseph Forgives His Brothers Genesis 37-45

Lesson: God wants us to forgive others.

When Joseph arrived in Egypt, he was sold to an Egyptian named Potiphar who worked for the king. Although Potiphar liked Joseph, he threw him in prison after Potiphar's wife told him lies about Joseph. One day the king called upon Joseph to interpret a dream he had. Joseph explained to the king that Egypt would have seven years of abundant food, followed by seven years of famine in the land. He suggested that the king store up grain in the plentiful years, so that the people could eat when there was little food. The king was impressed with Joseph and put him in charge of storing food.

When there was no food in Canaan, Jacob told his sons to go to Egypt to buy food. When they arrived in Egypt they did not recognize their brother Joseph. Although his brothers sold him as a slave many years before, Joseph had compassion on his brothers and forgave them. God took care of Joseph during this difficult time. You can read more about Joseph and his brothers in Genesis 42-46.

Forgiveness

Make bread to share with others

Ingredients:

- 2 cups warm water (roughly 100 degrees)
- 2/3 cup white sugar
- 1 ½ tablespoons active dry yeast
- 1 ½ teaspoons salt
- ¼ cup vegetable oil
- 6 cups bread flour
- Cooking oil spray

Also:

- Large bowl
- Mixing cups
- Measuring spoons
- Cookie sheet (or bread pan)

Directions:

1. Kids love to knead dough but wash hands first.
2. In a large bowl dissolve the sugar in the warm water and stir in the yeast. Allow the yeast to become foamy.
3. Mix in salt and flour. Flour is best one cup at a time. Knead the dough in the bowl until smooth. Put the dough in an oiled bowl and cover with a damp cloth. Let rise for at least an hour or until it doubles in size.
4. Knead dough again and divide in 2 halves. Form a shape with the dough or braid it and place on cookie sheet sprayed with cooking oil. Let rise again for about ½ hour.
5. Bake at 350 degrees for 30 minutes.
6. Serve warm.

Daniel in the Lions' Den Daniel 6:1–22

Lesson: God answers our prayers.

Daniel loved God and prayed to Him everyday. King Darius liked Daniel and wanted to put him in charge of his entire kingdom. But other leaders did not want Daniel to be in charge, so they came up with a plan. They told the king, "O King Darius, we think you should make a law. It should say if anyone prays to a god other than your god they will be thrown into the lions' den." The king agreed. When Daniel heard about the new law, he went home and prayed to God. The other leaders found Daniel praying and told King Darius. The king liked Daniel and was very upset. But he had made the law and ordered Daniel to be thrown into the lions' den. The king said, "May your God save you!" All night the king worried about Daniel. The king did not eat or sleep. God sent an angel to protect Daniel. God shut the mouths of all the lions. The next morning, King Darius ran to the lions' den. He found Daniel safe and unharmed. Daniel shouted, "My God sent His angel and He shut the lions' mouths." King Darius was happy and ordered everyone in the kingdom to pray to Daniel's God.

Prayer Can or Jar

Materials Needed:

- Jar such as peanut butter or coffee jar, (or plastic jar from craft store)
- Paper
- Pens or markers
- Construction paper

Instructions:

1. Write out prayers and roll into scrolls, place in jar.
2. Decorate jar as desired.
3. Take out and read a prayer a day.

Baby Moses Exodus 2:1–10

Lesson: God will keep me safe.

When Pharaoh became the new king of Egypt, he did not like that the Israelites were having a lot of babies. He feared that one day they would take over Egypt. So he made a new law saying that any new baby boy born to an Israelite family would be killed. What a horrible mean law. An Israelite woman had a baby boy and hid him for many months. When she could no longer hide him, she made a basket and placed him in the Nile River. When Pharaoh's daughter came to bathe in the river, she saw the baby and wanted to protect him. Because Miriam, the baby boy's sister was watching, she asked Pharaoh's daughter if she would like for an Israelite mother to take care of the baby. Pharaoh's daughter said yes, so the baby boy's mother ended up nursing and taking care of her son. Pharaoh's daughter named the baby boy Moses.

Weave a Basket

Make a straw-type basket

Materials Needed:

- Straw or gift basket filler
- Pipe cleaners
- Construction paper
- Glue
- Baby doll - optional

Instructions:

1. Form the filler into a basket with your hands.
2. Put pipe cleaners through the sides to form the handles.
3. Glue to construction paper so basket doesn't fall apart.
4. (optional – add a baby doll to the basket).

The Burning Bush

Exodus 3:1–10

Lesson: I will listen to God.

Even though Moses grew up in the beautiful Egyptian palace, he knew that he was an Israelite. He felt sorry for the Israelite slaves because the Egyptians treated them harshly. One day, he killed an Egyptian slave master when he was beating an Israelite. When Pharaoh found out, he wanted Moses killed. Moses fled Egypt and went to the land of Midian.

One day while Moses was watching his sheep he saw a burning bush. As he approached the bush God said, "Do not come any closer. Take off your sandals because you are standing on holy ground." Moses obeyed God. Then God said, "...And now the cry of the Israelites has reached me, and I have seen the way the Egyptians are oppressing them. So now, go. I am sending you to Pharaoh to bring my people the Israelites out of Egypt."

Moses was hesitant. He said to God," Who am I, that I should go to Pharaoh and bring the Israelites out of Egypt?" And God said, "I will be with you." Moses did not think he could do what God asked. He felt uncomfortable and not worthy of the task given to him. But he went anyway, believing God would be with him. Moses listened to God.

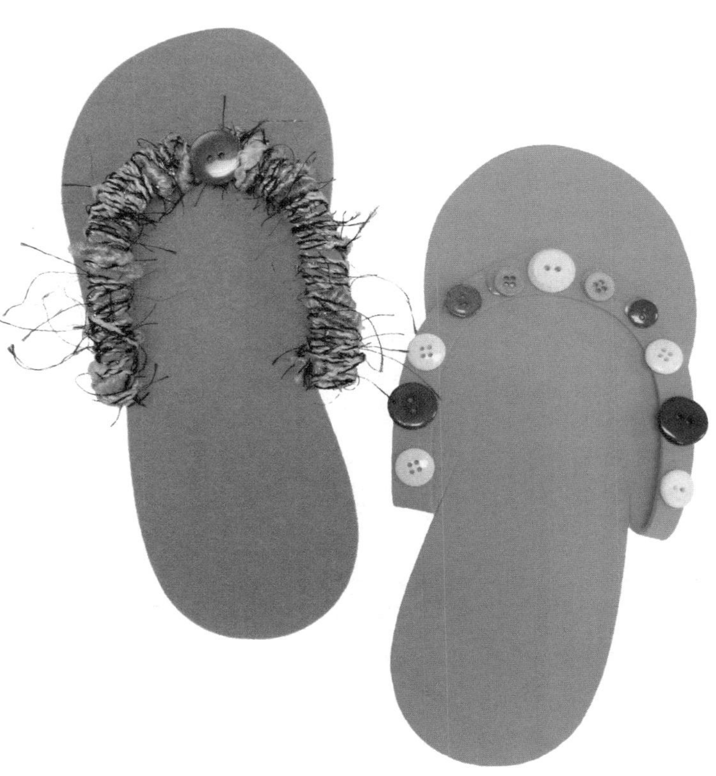

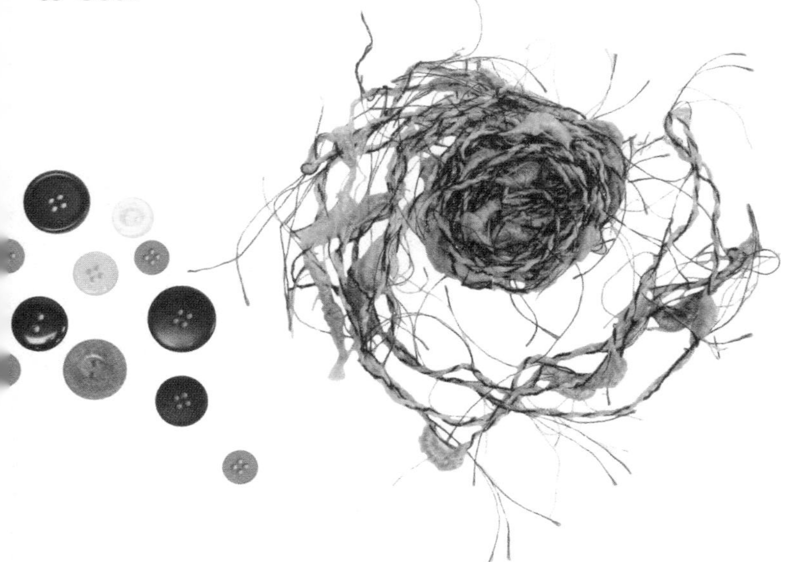

Sandals

Materials Needed:

- Sandal pattern or flip flops from beauty supply store or Dollar Store
- Glue
- Construction paper or tag board
- Decorations (use whatever you have at home such as buttons, jewels, construction paper, yarn, etc.)

Instructions:

1. Cut out pattern to fit feet or use sandals from supply center.
2. If using pattern, make sandal straps from masking tape or construction paper.
3. Decorate as desired!

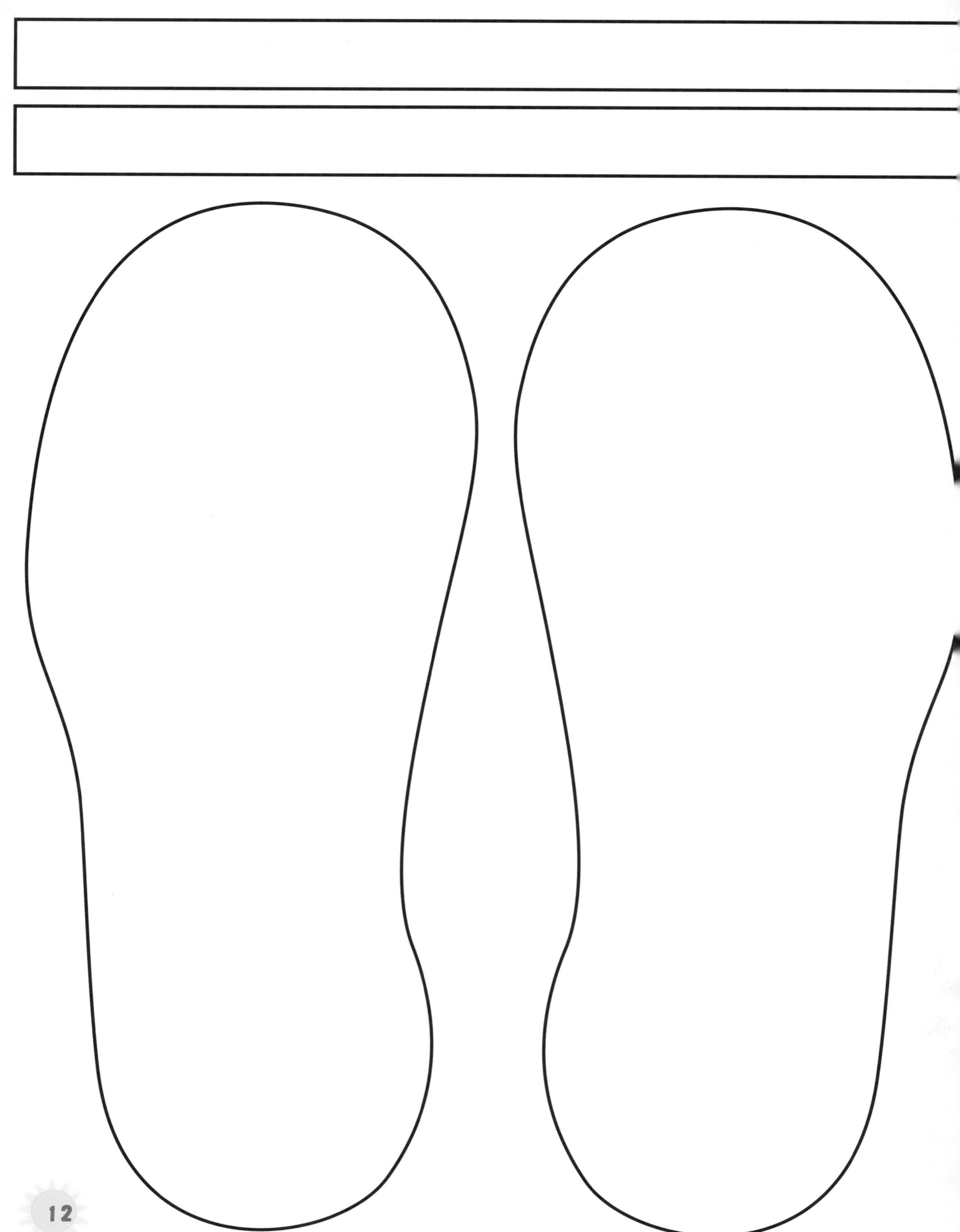

The Story of Joshua

Joshua 6:20

Lesson: God's way is the best way for me!

A very tall wall surrounded the city of Jericho. God had told Joshua to get his soldiers ready to fight the city. But how would they get through the large stone wall? God had a plan. He told Joshua to have his army march around the city each day. His army marched around the city for six days. On the seventh day, God told Joshua to have his army march around the wall seven times. On the seventh time the priests sounded the trumpet blast. Joshua commanded the people, "Shout! For the Lord has given you the city." The walls of Jericho came tumbling down. Joshua's army had won the battle. God knows what is best. Joshua listened to God.

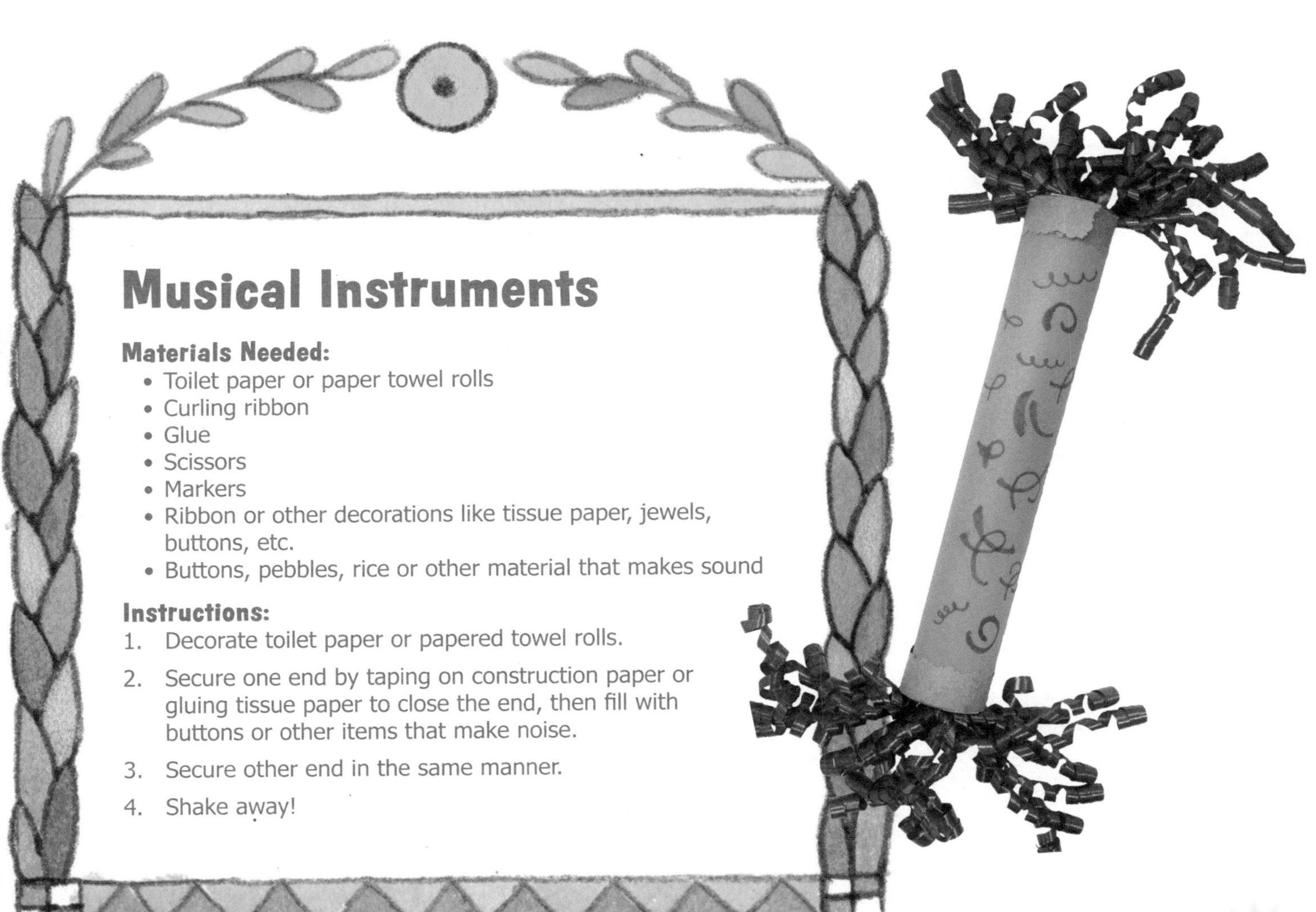

Musical Instruments

Materials Needed:

- Toilet paper or paper towel rolls
- Curling ribbon
- Glue
- Scissors
- Markers
- Ribbon or other decorations like tissue paper, jewels, buttons, etc.
- Buttons, pebbles, rice or other material that makes sound

Instructions:

1. Decorate toilet paper or papered towel rolls.
2. Secure one end by taping on construction paper or gluing tissue paper to close the end, then fill with buttons or other items that make noise.
3. Secure other end in the same manner.
4. Shake away!

The Story of Ruth

Ruth

Lesson: God wants us to love and be kind to others.

Naomi and her husband Elimelech lived in Judah, but there was not enough food. They decided to take their two sons and move to the land of Moab. In Moab, both of Naomi's sons married, but then Naomi's husband and both of her sons died. She was very sad. She missed her family back in Judah. Naomi's daughter-in-laws, Orpah and Ruth, felt sorry for Naomi. Ruth was tender-hearted and wanted to stay with Naomi. She followed Naomi back to her home in Judah. She took care of Naomi and made sure she had food to eat. God blessed Ruth for her kindness and provided her with a husband named Boaz. Soon they had a baby boy named Obed. They were happy. God took care of Naomi and Ruth.

Make a Hanging Heart to Hold Bible Verses

Materials Needed:

- Construction paper
- Yarn or curling ribbon
- Scissors
- Hole punch
- Markers

Instructions:

1. Cut out 2 hearts from construction paper.
2. For the bottom heart cut straight across slightly more than halfway up.
3. Hole punch around both hearts together.
4. Sew with yarn or curling ribbon.
5. Add a top loop with yarn from both sides in the same hole in order to balance and to make the hanging loop.
6. Decorate as desired.
7. Add memory verse strips.
8. Pull out as needed to practice memorization.

Scripture Memory

Scripture Verses

I will praise you, O LORD, with all my heart; I will tell of all your wonders.

Psalm 9:1

Trust in the LORD with all your heart and lean not on your own understanding; in all your ways acknowledge him, and he will make your paths straight.

Proverbs 3:5-6

For God so loved the world that he gave his one and only Son, that whoever believes in him shall not perish but have eternal life.

John 3:16

The LORD your God is with you, he is mighty to save. He will take great delight in you, he will quiet you with his love, he will rejoice over you with singing.

Zephaniah 3:17

For it is by grace you have been saved, through faith– and this not from yourselves, it is the gift of God.

Ephesians 2:8

Love the LORD your God with all your heart and with all your soul and with all your strength.

Deuteronomy 6:5

That is you confess with your mouth, "Jesus is Lord," and believe in your heart that God raised him from the dead, you will be saved.

Romans 10:9

I love you , O LORD, my strength.

Psalm 18:1

Scripture Verses

You will go out in joy and be led forth in peace; the mountains and hills will burst into song before you, and all the trees of the field will clap their hands.

Isaiah 55:12

Do not conform any longer to the pattern of this world, but be transformed by the renewing of your mind. Then you will be able to test and approve what God's will is—his good, pleasing and perfect will.

Romans 12:2

Great is the LORD and most worthy of praise; his greatness no one can fathom.

Psalm 145:3

Be completely humble and gentle; be patient, bearing with one another in love.

Ephesians 4:2

From the fullness of his grace we have all received one blessing after another.

John 1:16

Accept one another, then, just as Christ accepted you, in order to bring praise to God.

Romans 15:7

Now faith is being sure of what we hope for and certain of what we do not see.

Hebrews 11:1

This is love: not that we loved God, but that he loved us and sent his Son as an atoning sacrifice for our sins.

1 John 4:10

David The Shepherd Boy Psalm 23

Lesson: The Lord is my shepherd; He watches over me.

David loved God. When he became king after Saul died, David prayed to God for wisdom and trusted Him. One of the most well known songs that David wrote is Psalm 23.

The Lord is my shepherd, I shall
not be in want.
He makes me lie down in green
pastures,
he leads me beside quiet waters,
he restores my soul.
He guides me in paths of
righteousness
for his name's sake.
Even though I walk
through the valley of the shadow of
death,
I will fear no evil,
for you are with me;
your rod and your staff,
they comfort me.

You prepare a table before me
in the presence of my enemies.
You anoint my head with oil;
my cup overflows.
Surely goodness and love will follow
me
all the days of my life,
and I will dwell in the house of the
LORD
forever.

Psalm 23

Make Sheep!

Materials Needed:

- Pattern
- Crayons or markers
- Scissors
- Popsicle sticks
- Glue
- Cotton balls

Instructions:

1. Color pattern and cut out.
2. Cut cotton balls in small pieces and roll in the palm of your hand to make small cotton balls.
3. Glue to pattern.
4. Glue pattern to popsicle stick.
5. For the back, use the other pattern.

This craft is PERFECT
for young children!

Jonah and the Whale

Jonah

Lesson: God answers our prayers!

One day God said to Jonah, "I want you to go to the city of Ninevah and tell the people to stop doing bad things." But Jonah was afraid. He did not want to go to Ninevah. So Jonah ran away. Jonah boarded a ship that would sail far from Ninevah. While Jonah was sleeping, God sent a forceful storm. The sailors were afraid. Jonah knew that the storm was his fault because he did not obey the Lord's command. Jonah told the sailors to throw him overboard. The sailors did not want to, but the storm was getting worse. As soon as the sailors threw Jonah into the water, the sea grew calm. God sent a big fish to swallow Jonah.

Jonah was inside the big fish for three days and three nights. He was sorry he did not listen to God. He prayed and asked God for forgiveness. God told the fish to spit Jonah out onto dry land. Jonah immediately went to the city of Ninevah. He told the people about God. They were sorry for the bad things they had done. The people asked God to forgive them and God did!

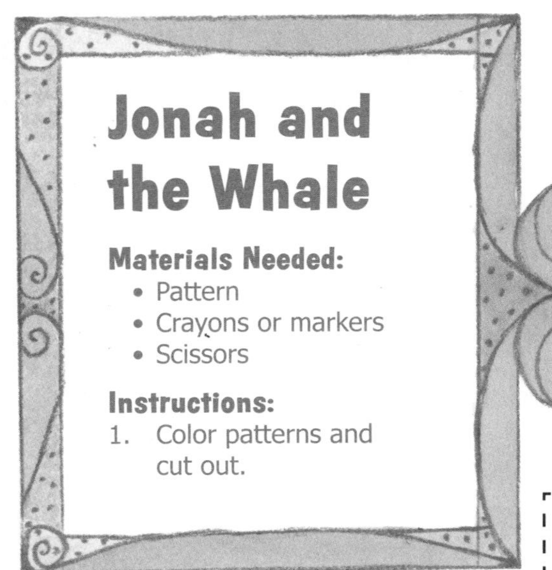

Have children retell the story of Jonah and The Whale in their own words!

A Special Angel Luke 1:26-38

Lesson: Mary trusted God. I will trust God, too!

Mary was a very special young woman who loved God. One day an angel named Gabriel came to Mary and told her she was going to have a baby. Mary was afraid because she did not think this was possible. Mary was not married at that time. The angel said, "Do not be afraid, Mary, you have found favor with God. You will have a child and give birth to a son, and you are to give him the name Jesus." Mary did not understand. But Mary trusted God.

Angel

Materials Needed

- Patterns
- Scissors
- Tape
- 4 basket coffee filters
- Construction paper (any color you choose)
- Black marker
- Crayons or markers
- Glitter glue (optional)
- Ribbon (optional)
- Glue

Instructions

- Color pattern and cut out.
- Take 2 different colors of construction paper and cut in half.
- Cut out the half circle patterns and trace onto the construction paper. Cut out shapes and roll each into a cone shape. Tape together in the back, one at a time.
- Take 2 coffee filters and overlap them, then tape to the back of the cone to make the wings for each angel.
- Glue the arms on each side of the cone and fold slightly so they stand out.
- Glue the head and halo onto the front top of the cone.
- Decorate!

Jesus Is Born Luke 2

Lesson: Nothing is impossible with God.

Mary and Joseph traveled to Bethlehem. Mary rode on a donkey. Soon after they arrived Mary told Joseph it was time for the baby to be born. But there was no room at the inn. Finally, Joseph found a stable. Among the horses, cows, and sheep the baby Jesus was born. The animals must have been surprised. Mary gently wrapped Jesus in cloths and placed Him in a manger. The angels praised God saying, "Glory to God in the highest!"

Make the nativity scene together as a family and display in your home. Encourage your children to retell the story of Jesus' birth and read Luke Chapter 2 together.

Make a Nativity Scene

Materials Needed:

- Pattern
- Crayons or markers
- Scissors

Instructions:

- Color pattern and cut out.
- Fold on the dotted lines and tape together figures will stand up.

Wise Men Come To Worship Matthew 2:1–12

Lesson: God gave us the gift of his son Jesus!

The wise men looked up into the eastern sky and saw the most brilliant, bright star. They had never seen such a beautiful star so they followed it night after night. The star stopped over the place where Jesus was and the wise men were overjoyed! They saw Jesus and Mary and bowed down to worship Him. Then they opened their treasures and presented Him with gifts. What gift would you bring to the baby Jesus? Can you imagine finding Jesus because a star helped you find the way? God is so creative, isn't He?

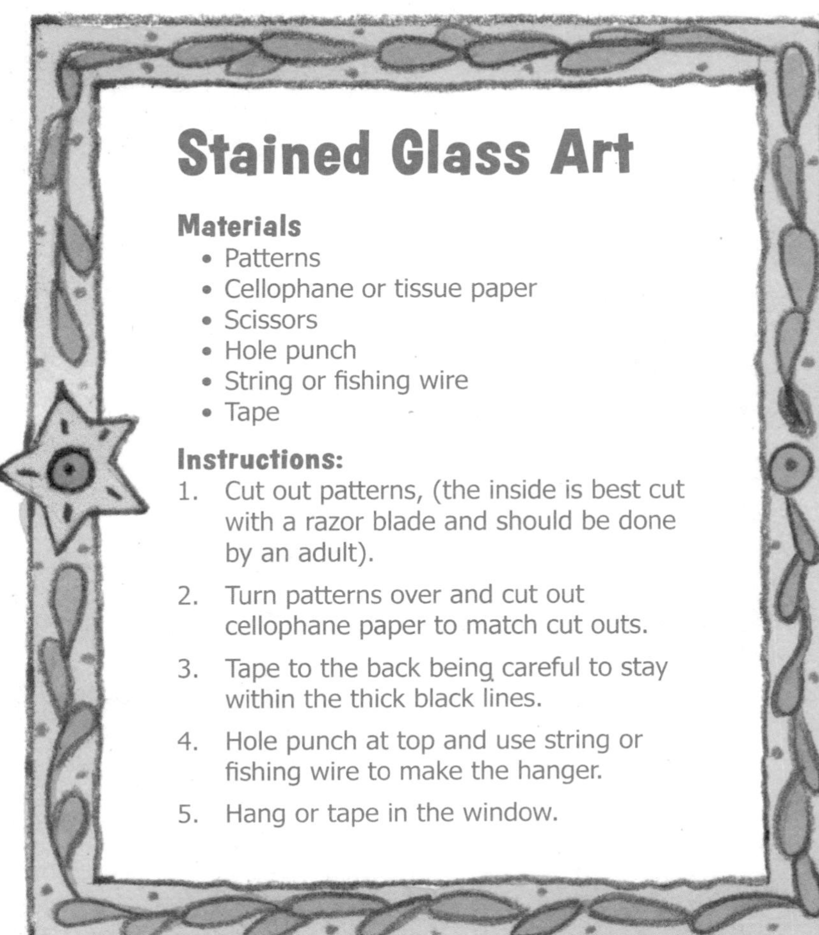

Stained Glass Art

Materials

- Patterns
- Cellophane or tissue paper
- Scissors
- Hole punch
- String or fishing wire
- Tape

Instructions:

1. Cut out patterns, (the inside is best cut with a razor blade and should be done by an adult).
2. Turn patterns over and cut out cellophane paper to match cut outs.
3. Tape to the back being careful to stay within the thick black lines.
4. Hole punch at top and use string or fishing wire to make the hanger.
5. Hang or tape in the window.

Young children can color with crayon or marker instead!

Make your own star
for this activity and
decorate an
entire window!

Jesus Calls His Disciples Matthew 4:18–21

Lesson: Jesus wants us to follow Him everyday.

One day Jesus was walking beside the Sea of Galilee and He saw two brothers. They were casting their nets into the lake because they were fishermen. Jesus called out to Peter and Andrew, "Come follow me and I will make you fishers of men." They immediately threw down their nets and followed Jesus. Jesus needed other helpers too. He saw James and his brother John preparing their nets with their father Zebedee. When Jesus called out to them, they left their nets and their father and followed Jesus. Jesus went through Galilee teaching people about God and healing the sick. He loved His disciples and told them how to treat people and all about the kingdom of God. Jesus had twelve disciples.

Fish Mobile

Materials Needed:

- Patterns
- Crayons or markers
- Scissors
- Hanger
- Fishing wire or string
- Hole punch
- Tape

Instructions:

1. Color patterns and cut out.
2. Write the names of the disciples in marker on the fish.
3. Hole punch fish and string to make mobile.
4. Tape sign to the hanger.

Jesus' Twelve Disciples

Matthew 10: 2-4

"These are the names of the twelve apostles: first Simon (who is called Peter) and his brother Andrew; James son of Zebedee, and his brother John; Philip and Bartholomew; Thomas and Matthew the tax collector; James son of Alphaeus, and Thaddaeus; Simon the Zealot and Judas Iscariot, who betrayed him."

I WILL MAKE
YOU FISHERS
OF MEN

Lesson: Jesus loves me!

Jesus loved people and He especially loved children. Parents would bring their children to Jesus so that Jesus could heal them. Or, they would just want their children to sit on Jesus' lap so He could touch them and bless them. Jesus was always so loving and patient. One day when the children were brought to Jesus for Him to place his hands on them and pray for them, His disciples got angry. They wanted the children to leave. But Jesus said, "Do not tell the children to leave. Let the little children come to me." Jesus would tell wonderful stories to the children and teach them about God.

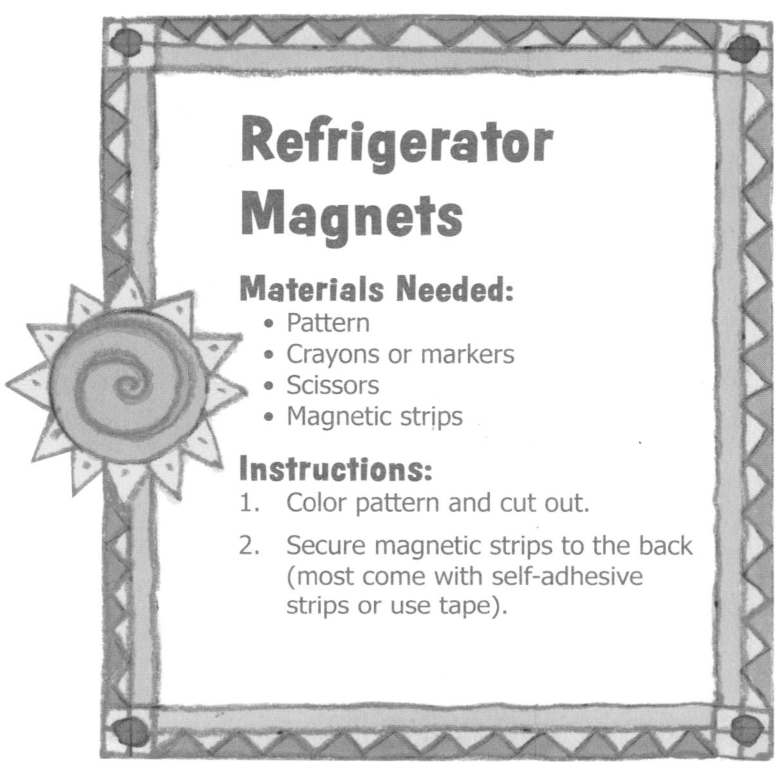

Refrigerator Magnets

Materials Needed:

- Pattern
- Crayons or markers
- Scissors
- Magnetic strips

Instructions:

1. Color pattern and cut out.
2. Secure magnetic strips to the back (most come with self-adhesive strips or use tape).

JESUS
LOVES ME
JESUS
LOVES ME
I AM A CHILD OF
JESUS
The Lord
is my
SHEPHERD

Jesus Feeds 5,000

Matthew 14:13-21,
Mark 6:30-44,
Luke 9:10-17

Lesson: Jesus will supply all of my needs.

When Jesus talked to people, large crowds would gather to listen. Jesus would pray with them and heal the sick. One day when Jesus was healing people it started to get dark. His disciples were concerned and told Jesus to tell the crowd to go to the village to buy food. Jesus replied, "They do not need to go away. You give them something to eat." "We only have five loaves of bread and two fish," they answered. That did not concern Jesus. Jesus said, "Bring them here to me." He told the people to sit down on the grass. Then Jesus took the five loaves and two fish and looking up to heaven, he gave thanks and broke the loaves. Jesus gave His disciples the food and they gave the food to all of the people. When everyone had enough to eat the disciples gathered twelve basketfuls that were left over. Jesus fed over 5,000 people that day!

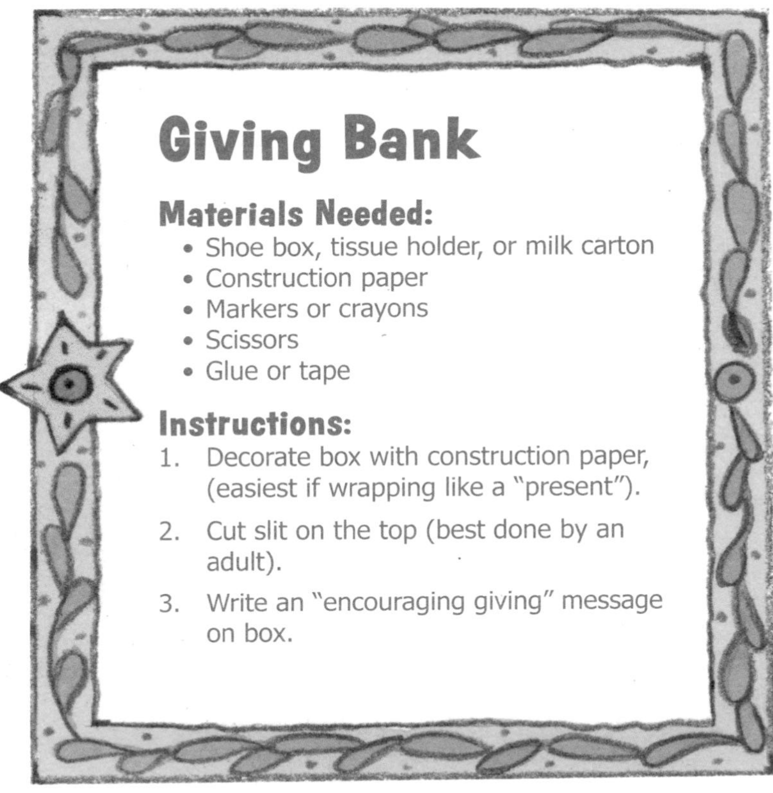

Giving Bank

Materials Needed:

- Shoe box, tissue holder, or milk carton
- Construction paper
- Markers or crayons
- Scissors
- Glue or tape

Instructions:

1. Decorate box with construction paper, (easiest if wrapping like a "present").
2. Cut slit on the top (best done by an adult).
3. Write an "encouraging giving" message on box.

Jesus Dies

Matthew 27: 35-50, Mark 15:21-37, Luke 23:33-43, John 19:17-37

Lesson: Jesus died for my sins.

Jesus loved to tell people about God. Jesus told them that He would die and that He would live again. Jesus died on a cross because people did not believe He was God's Son. Friends of Jesus placed His body in a tomb. A large stone was rolled in front of the entrance. Soldiers guarded the tomb so that no one would take Jesus' body.

RED is for the blood Jesus shed.

GREEN is for new life ahead.

BLACK is for the sins we've made.

WHITE is for perfect grace He gave.

PURPLE is for His hour of sorrow.

PINK is for our new tomorrow

Cross Poem

Materials Needed:

- Pattern
- Glue
- Scissors
- Markers

Instructions:

1. Color heart on pattern.
2. Cut out squares and glue to the cross.

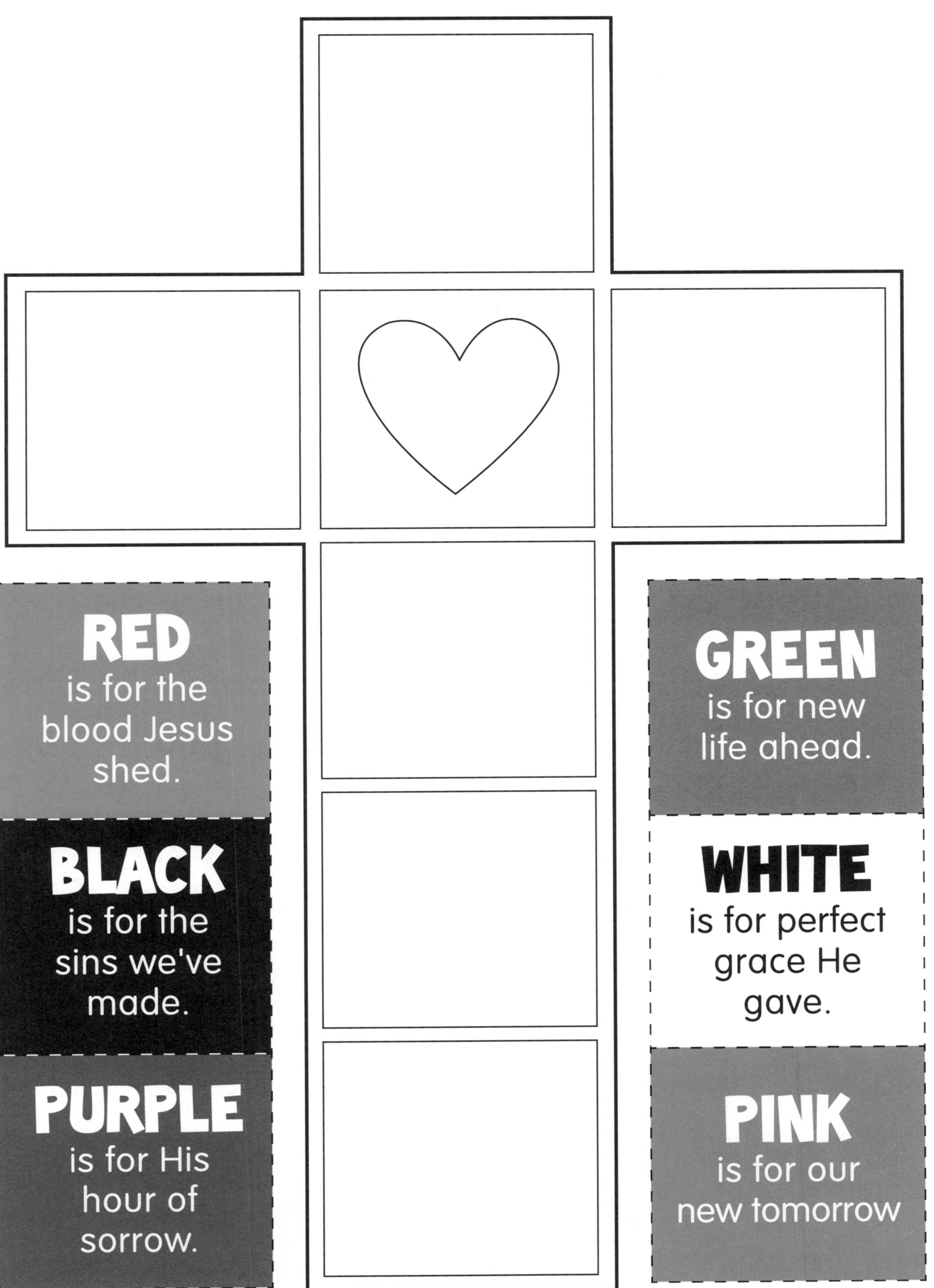

RED
is for the
blood Jesus
shed.
BLACK
is for the
sins we've
made.
PURPLE
is for His
hour of
sorrow.
GREEN
is for new
life ahead.
WHITE
is for perfect
grace He
gave.
PINK
is for our
new tomorrow

Jesus is Alive

Matthew 28:5-7
Luke 24:1-12

Lesson: Jesus died and rose again for me!

The next day, two women both named Mary, came to the tomb. They found the stone rolled away from the entrance. An angel sitting on the stone said, "Jesus is not here! He is alive! Go quickly and tell His friends!" The women ran back to the others! "Jesus is alive!" He is risen!" shouted the women. The friends did not believe the women! Peter, one of Jesus' closest friends, ran to the tomb. He looked inside and found only the cloths that had wrapped Jesus' body! Later that day, Jesus joined two of His friends while they walked along the road to a little village. Then, Jesus visited the disciples in Jerusalem. He showed them His nail-scarred hands and feet! It was true–Jesus was alive! "Do you remember what I said to you?" asked Jesus. "I told you I would die and on the third day I would come back to life again. You have seen this happen!"

Door Hangers

Materials Needed:

- Pattern
- Crayons or markers
- Scissors

Instructions:

1. Color pattern and cut out.
2. Cut a slit to connect to the circle so there is an opening to hang on the door.

JESUS LIVES

Tell Everyone About Jesus Mark 16:15

Lesson: Jesus wants us to follow Him everyday!

Jesus told the most wonderful stories. He taught his disciples about God and he taught them how they should live their lives. Jesus also taught his disciples to share the story with everyone they knew and met. Jesus loves every man, woman, and child in the world so much that He wants EVERYONE to know about Him. Do you know how much God loves you? He loves you so much that He sent His only Son to die on the cross so that you might live with Him someday. You need to believe and trust God. God's plan is perfect!

Wrist Bands

Materials Needed:

- Patterns
- Crayons or markers
- Scissors
- Tape

Instructions:

1. Color patterns and cut out.
2. Make a circle with the bands and tape securely.

JESUS ♡ JESUS ♡ JESUS ♡ JESUS

FOR GOD SO LOVED THE WORLD

Philippians 4:13

God Rocks My World!

I'm a follower of Christ

ASK ME ABOUT JESUS